I0105919

The Little Black Book of

Birthday Wisdom

Quotes on Aging, Life, and Birthday Cake

Mike Kowis, Esq.

THE LITTLE BLACK BOOK OF BIRTHDAY WISDOM:

Quotes on Aging, Life, and Birthday Cake

by Mike Kowis, Esq.

Copyright © 2024 Mike Kowis, Esq.

All rights reserved. No part of this book may be reproduced or transmitted in any form or by any means, electronic or mechanical, including photocopying, recording, or by any information storage and retrieval system, without the written permission of the publisher except where permitted by law.

DISCLAIMER NOTICE: The quotes contained in this book are intended for educational and entertainment purposes only. No warranties of any kind are expressed or implied. By reading this book, the reader acknowledges that the author and publisher are not engaged in the rendering of tax, legal, or financial advice and further agrees that under no circumstances is the author or publisher responsible for any losses, direct or indirect, which are incurred as a result of the use of the information contained in this book, including, but not limited to, errors, omissions, or inaccuracies.

Library of Congress Control Number: 2024907317

ISBN-13: 979-8-9900133-3-9 (paperback)

ISBN-13: 979-8-9900133-2-2 (eBook)

www.mikekowis.com

Lecture PRO Publishing

Conroe, Texas

Dedication

This book is dedicated to all loving moms and dads because birthdays would simply not exist without them. May God bless each and every parent who was brave enough to bring a precious child into the world.

Dedication

Testimonials

Here's what people are saying about *The Little Black Book of Birthday Wisdom*:

> **Mike is the perfect person to write a book about birthdays... Lord knows he's had enough of them.** – *Mike's bartender*

> **Wow... this is Mike's tenth book! Obviously, he believes in quantity over quality.** – *Mike's accountant*

> **What does Mike know about milestone birthdays? He thought Sweet 16 was a sugar substitute.** – *Mike's offshore fishing guide*

> **I'm not saying Mike's new book was done in poor taste, but he put the PRO in INAPPROPRIATE.** – *Mike's psychiatrist*

> **This is the BEST BOOK I've ever read from a lobotomy patient.** – *Mike's dentist*

> **The title of this book contains the word "little," but that's not the only thing little about Mike.** – *IQ test administrator*

> ***The Little Black Book of Birthday Wisdom* is the perfect example of how NOT to write a book.** – *Mike's barber*

> **Maybe Mike should try writing a book in a foreign language... and then move to that country.** – *Mike's disappointed wife*

But seriously, you're gonna enjoy the following collection of amusing birthday quotes. Let's just hope they are more entertaining than the silly testimonials above!

Contents

INTRODUCTION

> **Every year on your birthday, you get a chance to start new.**
> — *Sammy Hagar*

Hard to admit, but I finally joined the HALF-CENTURY CLUB. That means I completed at least 50 trips around the Sun and lived to tell about it. Despite my fears, I found that turning 50 years old was not so bad once I got used to eating dinner at 4:30 pm and yelling at teenagers to stay off my lawn. But seriously, hitting the big five-oh made me feel grateful for the precious gift of life and appreciate the opportunity to share another day with friends and family.

This momentous occasion also made me think deeply about the annual celebration of life commonly known as a birthday. What is it really and why is it treated differently than any other day? Is it just an ingenious marketing campaign devised by the greeting card industry or is there a profound reason why people track their years on earth? Are there any spiritual or religious teachings about this special day? Why do so many people dread their next birthday? We all grapple with these burning questions from time to time. To anyone contemplating your next birthday and what it means to add another candle on top of your cake, take heart! You might find some of the answers in this silly book filled with 501 humorous and thought-provoking quotes about aging, life, and birthday cake.

The quotations below touch on a wide variety of concepts related to birthdays, including well-known sayings, toasts, jokes, milestone birthdays, religious teachings, and much more. Each chapter covers a different topic, but there is a degree of overlap.

Following this Introduction, Chapters 1 through 3 include famous sayings, humorous quotes, and birthday toasts, respectively. In addition to Chapter 2, you'll find funny quips sprinkled throughout the entire book.

Chapter 4 discusses all things related to candles and cake, and Chapter 5 explores the concept of gifts. Next, Chapters 6 touches on milestone birthdays – which are significant birthdays such as sweet 16, adulthood (18), and over-the-hill (40).

Chapters 7, 8, and 9 cover youth, seasoned citizens, and comparisons between the two, respectively. Chapter 10 explains many peoples' fear of birthdays, which is also known as "Fragapanophobia." Try saying that five times fast!

Chapter 11 shares spiritual teachings about birthdays, while Chapter 12 includes sayings that didn't fit neatly elsewhere. Finally, the Conclusion distills the following quotations into a handful of salient points and shares my top ten list.

I hope you enjoy the following birthday quotes as much as I enjoyed gathering them. Happy reading – and you can quote me on that!

CHAPTER 1

Famous Sayings

There are two great days in a person's life – the day we are born and the day we discover why.
– *William Barclay*

Today you are you! That is truer than true! There is no one alive who is you-er than you!

– *Dr. Seuss, Happy Birthday to You! (1959)*

Do not complain about growing old. It is a privilege denied to many.

– *Mark Twain*

Growing old is mandatory; growing up is optional.

– *Chili Davis*

The way I see it, you should live every day like it's your birthday.

— *Paris Hilton*

The greatest thing in life is to die young – but delay it as long as possible.

— *George Bernard Shaw*

We do not count a man's years until he has nothing else to count.

— *Ralph Waldo Emerson*

How old would you be if you didn't know how old you are?

— *Satchel Paige*

We turn not older with years, but newer every day.

— *Emily Dickinson*

Men are like wine: some turn to vinegar, but the best improve with age.

— *Pope John XXIII*

Age is a case of mind over matter. If you don't mind, it doesn't matter.

— *Mark Twain*

A diplomat is a man who always remembers a woman's birthday, but never remembers her age.

— *Robert Frost*

Childhood itself is scarcely more lovely than a cheerful, kindly, sunshiny old age.

— *Lydia M. Child*

The more you praise and celebrate your life, the more there is in life to celebrate.

— *Oprah Winfrey*

Come grow old with me. The best is yet to be.

— *William Wordsworth*

We don't stop playing because we grow old; we grow old because we stop playing.

— *George Bernard Shaw*

You don't get older, you get better.

— *Shirley Bassey*

A birth-date is a reminder to celebrate the life as well as to update the life.

— *Amit Kalantri*

Deep down, I believe my year was a special year: it produced me.

— *Ned Vizzini*

Birthday is the day to take a pause and live the day for yourself. It's a day to look back at the miles (years) walked so far and plan the next miles of dreams to change your life and others too.

— *Vikrmn: CA Vikram Verma, Slate (2022)*

Age is whatever you think it is. You are as old as you think you are.

— *Muhammad Ali*

What could be more beautiful than a dear old lady growing wise with age? Every age can be enchanting, provided you live within it.

— *Brigitte Bardot*

Our birthdays are feathers in the broad wings of time.

— *Jean Paul Richter*

To me, a birthday means celebrating the presence of an individual in our lives.

— *Meena Bajaj*

<hr/>

We are always the same age inside.

— *Gertrude Stein*

<hr/>

A child whose birthday is coming up is so excited, they count down the days. But as we get older, we seem to lose the excitement. We need to rethink and be happy we have reached another birthday.

— *Theodore W. Higginsworth*

<hr/>

Most of us can remember a time when a birthday – especially if it was one's own – brightened the world as if a second sun has risen.

— *Robert Staughton Lynd*

<hr/>

Age is just a number, not a state of mind or a reason for any type of particular behavior.

— *Cecelia Ahern, Love, Rosie (2004)*

<hr/>

Aging seems to be the only available way to live a long life.

— *Kitty Collins*

<hr/>

We normally know we're getting older when the only thing we want for our birthday is not to be reminded; unless you're a cancer survivor, then we love being reminded!

— *Chris Geiger, The Cancer Survivors Club: A Collection of Inspirational and Uplifting Stories (2012)*

❦

You can have a spiritual awakening and discover a new side of you at any age. And best of all, love can happen at any age. Life can just start to get exciting when you're in your 40s and 50s. You have to believe that.

— *Salma Hayek*

❦

I love the big fresh starts, the clean slates like birthdays and New Years, but I also really like the idea that we can get up every morning and start over.

— *Kristin Armstrong*

❦

Aging is not "lost youth," but a new stage of opportunity and strength.

— *Betty Friedan*

❦

Let us never know what old age is. Let us know the happiness time brings, not count the years.

— *Ausonius*

❦

Your birthday is your personal New Year's Day. This is the season to courageously reassess, release, and reset.

— *Robin S. Baker*

Birthdays are inevitable, beautiful and very particular moments in our lives! Moments that bring precious memories back, celebrate the present times and give hope for the future.

— *Babe Arish*

I think all this talk about age is foolish. Every time I'm one year older, everyone else is too.

— *Gloria Swanson*

Nature gives you the face you have at 20, but it's up to you to merit the face you have at 50.

— *Coco Chanel*

Each ten years of a man's life has its own fortunes, its own hopes, its own desires.

— *Johann Wolfgang von Goethe*

I was honored when they asked me to appear at the president's birthday rally in Madison Square Garden. There was like a hush over the whole place when I came on to sing "Happy Birthday," like if I had been wearing a slip, I would have thought it was showing or something. I thought, "Oh, my gosh, what if no sound comes out!"

– *Marilyn Monroe*

I believe that no matter what condition you are in when someone close to your heart remembers your birthday and wishes you a happy birthday, you feel happy.

– *A. Singla*

Why party like it is 1999 when you can party like it is your birthday?

– *Prince*

Success is like reaching an important birthday and finding you're exactly the same.

– *Audrey Hepburn*

I was forced to live far beyond my years when just a child, now I have reversed the order and I intend to remain young indefinitely.

– *Mary Pickford*

You take all the experience and judgment of men over 50 out of the world and there wouldn't be enough left to run it.

— Henry Ford

We should celebrate every year that we made it through and every year that we're happier and healthier.

— Ellen DeGeneres

Live not one's life as though one had a thousand years, but live each day as the last.

— Roman Emperor Marcus Aurelius

Life is a moderately good play with a badly written third act.

— Truman Capote

There is no cure for birth and death save to enjoy the interval.

— George Santayana

Old age isn't so bad when you consider the alternative.

— Maurice Chevalier

The first hundred years are the hardest.

— Wilson Mizner

CHAPTER 2

Wisecracks

There is still no cure for the common birthday.
— U.S. Senator and astronaut John Glenn

Something to remember on your birthday. Forget the past, it can't be changed. And, forget the present because I didn't get you one.

— Brian Jones

When a man has a birthday, he takes a day off. When a woman has a birthday, she takes at least three years off.

— Joan Rivers

Birthdays are good for you. Statistics show that the people who have the most live the longest.

— Larry Lorenzoni

As you get older, three things happen: The first is your memory goes, and I can't remember the other two.

— *Norman Wisdom*

Like many women my age, I am 28 years old.

— *Mary Schmich*

Everyone over 50 should be issued every week with a wet fish in a plastic bag by the Post Office so that, whenever you see someone young and happy, you can hit them as hard as you can across the face.

— *Richard Griffiths*

Don't worry about middle age: you'll outgrow it.

— *Laurence J. Peter*

Last year, my birthday cake looked like a prairie fire.

— *Rodney Dangerfield*

Yes, you're very, very old. But try to think of it as not being cursed. After all, in a hostage situation you'd be released first!

— *John Walter Bratton*

Telling me to relax or smile when I'm angry is like bringing a birthday cake into an ape sanctuary. You're just asking to get your nose and genitals bitten off.

— Amy Poehler

Thanks to modern medical advances such as antibiotics, nasal spray, and Diet Coke, it has become routine for people in the civilized world to pass the age of 40, sometimes more than once.

— Dave Barry

I'm at an age when my back goes out more than I do.

— Phyllis Diller

I occasionally get birthday cards from fans. But it's often the same message: They hope it's my last.

— Al Forman

I remember debating the finer points of flaky pastry with my chicken-pot-pie-obsessed American dad. I remember the divine mix of Thai food, TV dinners, and hearty, homemade goodness that have shaped this palate of mine to this day. I remember all this, but I still Google my husband's birthday. Thank God he's famous.

— Chrissy Teigen

Time and tide wait for no man, but time always stands still for a woman of 30.

  – *Robert Frost*

Age becomes reality when you hear someone refer to that attractive young woman standing next to the woman in the green dress, and you find that you're the one in the green dress.

  – *Lois Wyse*

I was brought up to respect my elders, so now I don't have to respect anybody.

  – *George Burns*

The older you get the better you get, unless you are a banana.

  – *Betty White*

At 91, every day is a birthday.

  – *Charlotte Rae*

To get back my youth I would do anything in the world, except take exercise, get up early, or be respectable.

  – *Oscar Wilde*

I believe in loyalty. When a woman reaches an age she likes, she should stick with it.

— *Eva Gabor*

✖

It's odd the things that people remember. Parents will arrange a birthday party, certain it will stick in your mind forever. You'll have a nice time, then two years later you'll be like, "There was a pony there? Really? And a clown with one leg?"

— *David Sedaris*

✖

Wisdom doesn't necessarily come with age. Sometimes age just shows up all by itself.

— *Tom Wilson*

✖

If you live to be one hundred, you've got it made. Very few people die past that age.

— *George Burns*

✖

Thank you for all the birthday wishes. It's brought a tear to my eye and a boner to my pants.

— *Jack Barakat*

✖

Thirty-five is a very attractive age. London society is full of women of the very highest birth who have, of their own free choice, remained thirty-five for years.

— *Oscar Wilde*

The older I grow, the more I distrust the familiar doctrine that age brings wisdom.

— *H.L. Mencken*

Old age is like a plane flying through a storm. Once you are aboard, there is nothing you can do about it.

— *Israeli Prime Minister Golda Meir*

Time flies like an arrow. Fruit flies like a banana.

— *Groucho Marx*

Looking 50 is great, if you're 60.

— *Joan Rivers*

People who go around advertising their birthday are douchebags.

— *Katja Millay, The Sea of Tranquility (2012)*

What most persons consider as virtue, after the age of 40, is simply a loss of energy.

— *Voltaire*

Every year on my birthday, I start a new playlist titled after my current age so I can keep track of my favorite songs of the year as a sort of musical diary because I am a teenage girl.

— *Chris Hardwick*

Growing old is like being increasingly penalized for a crime you have not committed.

— *Anthony Powell*

Birthdays are a great time to stop and appreciate gravity. Sure, it makes things sag as you get older, but it also keeps your cake from flying all over the room, so you don't have to chase it.

— *Greg Tamblyn*

Death smells like birthday cake.

— *Maggie Stiefvater*

How young can you die of old age?

— *Steven Wright*

Interventions are really emotionally exhausting, and I would never ever want to have one. In the same way, I would never want to have a surprise birthday party. That would be horrible.

— *Margaret Cho*

In Hollywood, there is another name for a woman's 40th birthday party. It's a retirement party.

— *Artie Lange*

At 50, don't let aging get you down. It's too hard to get back up.

— *British Prime Minister H.H. Asquith*

Older people shouldn't eat health food, they need all the preservatives they can get.

— *Robert Orben*

If your Birthday is on Christmas day and you're not Jesus, you should start telling people your birthday is on June 9 or something. Just read up on the traits of a Gemini. Suddenly you're a multitasker who loves the color yellow. Because not only do you get stuck with them combo gift, you get the combo song. "We wish you a merry Christmas - and happy birthday, Terry - we wish you a merry Christmas - happy birthday, Terry - we wish you a merry Christmas and a happy New Ye - Birthday, Terry!

— *Ellen DeGeneres, Seriously... I'm Kidding (2011)*

The difference is, Jimmy was her husband and he's dead, and you're alive and you're a jackass.

That's real sweet, Daddy. Wish you'd saved it for my next birthday card.

— *Allie Ray, Children of Promise (2021)*

❧

If you want to look young and thin on your birthday, hang around a bunch of old fat people.

— *Anthony*

❧

For my birthday I got a humidifier and a de-humidifier. I put them in the same room and let them fight it out.

— *Steven Wright*

❧

I must confess, I was born at a very early age.

— *Groucho Marx*

❧

I was born full grown in the middle of a hurricane and an earthquake on 10 September 1954, 12.52 P.M. When I found out that I had missed lunch, I gave such a shout that the Earth stopped and spun backwards two days. That's why I celebrate my birthday on 8 September.

— *Jon Scieszka*

❧

I'm 60 years of age. That's 16 Celsius.

    — George Carlin

⚮

If you are an actress in L.A., on your 40th birthday they should just hand you the keys to the lunatic asylum.

    — Romola Garai

⚮

Your birthday reminds me of the old Chinese scholar… Yung No Mo.

    — European Parliament Member Dana Rosemary Scallon

⚮

Link says if a girl says not to get her a birthday present that means get me a birthday present and make sure it's jewelry.

    — Kami Garcia, Beautiful Creatures (2009)

⚮

I've got everything I had 20 years ago, except now it's all lower.

    — Gypsy Rose Lee

⚮

Nice to be here? At my age, it's nice to be anywhere.

    — George Burns

⚮

Few women admit their age. Few men act theirs.

    — U.S. Senator and astronaut John Glenn

⚮

CHAPTER 3

Toasts

> **May you live as long as you want and
> never want as long as you live.**
> *— Irish blessing*

May you live to be 100, and may the last voice you hear be mine.

— Frank Sinatra

With my wife, I don't get no respect. I made a toast on her birthday to "the best woman a man ever had." The waiter joined me.

— Rodney Dangerfield

Life seems to fade our memory, so on this birthday I will forget yours if you forget mine!

— Kate Summers

Today is the oldest you have been, and the youngest you will ever be. Make the most of it!

— *Nicky Gumbel*

❦

May you live all the days of your life.

— *Jonathan Swift*

❦

Birthday wishes are sent your way! To wish you such a wonderful day!

— *Julie McGregor*

❦

Live long and prosper.

— *Mr. Spock*

❦

In other words, live vicariously, beautifully, and excitingly, discover, love, dare and act as there is nothing to lose.

— *Andy Hertz*

❦

Pleas'd to look forward, pleas'd to look behind, and count each birthday with a grateful mind.

— *Alexander Pope*

❦

Today you have added another candle of knowledge and wisdom to your life. May it give you the power to enlighten the whole world. On your birthday, I wish you joy and happiness.

— *Dr. Debasish Mridha*

Another year comes to a close, and another begins. May the coming year be one that will be filled with laughter of friends, love of family, and the life that you dream of.

— *Catherine Pulsifer*

Today, you're halfway to 100! Here's to optimism, whether it is realistic or not.

— *T.S. Eliot*

You are never too old to set another goal or to dream a new dream.

— *Ohio Representative Les Brown*

May today be the best birthday of your life, I give you my heart as the most precious gift I can give you and I promise I always will love you.

— *Oscar Auliq-Ice*

Live your life so you don't have to have any regrets when you throw your 70-year-old birthday party.

– *Herdis Pala*

So mayst thou live, dear! Many years, in all the bliss that life endears.

– *Thomas Hood*

Don't just count your years, make your years count.

– *George Meredeth*

Birthdays come but once a year, celebrate and be of good cheer.

– *Robert Rivers*

Let all beings in all the worlds be happy. Include this universal prayer in your prayers every day. This is my birthday message to you.

– *Sathya Sai Baba*

May you receive many gifts, and may your day be joyous, and best of all may you be surrounded by family and friends. May all you wish for come true.

– *Theodore W. Higginsworth*

A birthday is like a new year and my wish for you, is a great year full of happiness and sunshine!

— *Catherine Pulsifer*

A birthday is like a new year and my wish for you, is a great year full of happiness and sunshine!

The day of your birthday is the one I expect the most in the year because I love to surprise you and do everything for us to enjoy wonderful moments together. God bless you today and always and may all your goals come true.

— *Oscar Auliq-Ice*

Your age isn't you. Use today to feel your best, celebrate and be your very happiest.

— *M. Rivers*

Today you are another year older, and we know how fast time flies as we get older, therefore, live each day and be happy!

— *Kate Summers*

May your birthday be as pleasant and awesome as you always are.

— *Dr. Debasish Mridha*

Celebrate your journey of life.

— *Lailah Gifty Akita*

Whatever with the past has gone, the best is always yet to come.

– Lucy Larcom

Let us celebrate the occasion with wine and sweet words.

– Plautus

CHAPTER 4

Candles & Cake

**You know you're getting old when the
candles cost more than the cake.**
— Bob Hope

Let them eat cake.

— French Queen Marie Antoinette

Put candles in a cake, it's a birthday cake. Put candles in a pie, and somebody's drunk in the kitchen.

— Jim Gaffigan

I remember when the candle shop burned down. Everyone stood around singing "Happy Birthday."

— Steven Wright

You can't say your favorite kind of cake is birthday cake. That's like saying your favorite kind of cereal is breakfast cereal.

    – Aziz Ansari

⚮

I explained birthday cake as a spongy mattress of awesome with hidden rivers of delicious goo to celebrate having stayed alive a whole year.

    – Kira Jane Buxton, Hollow Kingdom (2019)

⚮

The existence of birthday cake ice cream suggests that we can no longer distinguish celebration foods from everyday ones. We are also not too sure whether we are children or adults.

    – Bee Wilson, First Bite: How We Learn to Eat (2015)

⚮

My policy on cake is pro having it and pro eating it.

    – British Prime Minister Boris Johnson

⚮

All the world is birthday cake, so take a piece, but not too much.

    – George Harrison

⚮

At 50, if you are on a diet on your birthday, you can't eat a piece of your birthday cake. So grab two, a piece in each hand and, lo and behold, you will be on a balanced diet!

    – President Abraham Lincoln

⚮

I wanted to buy a candle holder, but the store didn't have one. So, I got a cake.

— *Mitch Hedberg*

✌

At her birthday, my seven-year-old daughter will say that she wants these big cakes and certain expensive toys as presents, and I can't say no to her. It would just break my heart. But when I was little, for birthdays we just played outside and we were happy if we got any cake.

— *Goran Ivanisevic*

✌

When the candles on your cake burn down before they are all lit you know you are getting up there.

— *Catherine Pulsifer*

✌

Most of us have fond memories of food from our childhood. Whether it was our mom's homemade lasagna or a memorable chocolate birthday cake, food has a way of transporting us back to the past.

— *Homaro Cantu*

✌

Cakes are special. Every birthday, every celebration ends with something sweet, a cake, and people remember. It's all about the memories.

— *Buddy Valastro*

✌

The cake had a book drawn on it, in icing. My mother, who had organized the party, told me that the lady at the bakery said that they had never put a book on a birthday cake before, and that mostly for boys it was footballs or spaceships. I was their first book.

– *Neil Gaiman*

Birthdays are nature's way of telling us to eat more cake.

– *Edward Morykwas*

You know you're getting old when you get that one candle on the cake. It's like, "See if you can blow this out."

– *Jerry Seinfeld*

Why is a birthday cake the only food you can blow on and spit on and everybody rushes to get a piece?

– *Bobby Kelton*

If life is a birthday cake, let my face be smeared with its icing of cognac and kindness.

– *Aberjhani*

Every day, every birthday candle I blow out, every penny I throw over my shoulder in a wishing well, every time my daughter says, "Let's make a wish on a star," there's one thing I wish for: wisdom.

— *Rene Russo*

Birthday marks the beginning of a new year, new hopes and new dreams! So, we should never blow out the candle before cutting the cake on such a day. Let the candle burn! Let it spread light everywhere!

— *Md. Ziaul Haque*

In a bar mitzvah, you do the candle-lighting ceremony with the cake. Every birthday, the cake is the big moment.

— *Ron Ben-Isreal*

Every year, I think you earn the right to eat cake on your birthday.

— *Bret Hart*

We was going to get you a birthday cake, but we figured you'd drop it.

— *Baseball Hall of Famer Casey Stengel*

Having a birthday cake squashed into your face by young kids? Delicious. I always don a Santa suit at Christmas. Remaining childish is a tremendous state of innocence.

    – *John Lydon*

∞

If you look over the years, the styles have changed - the clothes, the hair, the production, the approach to the songs. The icing to the cake has changed flavors. But if you really look at the cake itself, it's really the same.

    – *John Oates*

∞

You know what I think? I think that if a young woman doesn't engage in the act of occasionally wishing on a star or a flower or a birthday cake full of candles, then we're forfeiting one of the sweetest whimsies of our youth.

    – *Robin Jones Gunn*

∞

For me, the end of childhood came when the number of candles on my birthday cake no longer reflected my age, around 19 or 20. From then on, each candle came to represent an entire decade.

    – *Yotam Ottolenghi*

∞

I played with Buddy Guy on his 63rd birthday and got to bring him a cake. And I played with B.B. King on his 73rd birthday and got to bring him a cake, too.

— *Susan Tedeschi*

When someone asks if you'd like cake or pie, why not say you want cake and pie?

— *Lisa Loeb*

One of the best moments is right here (during History Tour in Copenhagen, on his birthday in 1997). Right here. It's right in the middle of the show and it's my birthday, and I'm thousands of miles away from my family. When they surprised me with the full marching band and then they brought out this huge, beautiful birthday cake, I realized that I've got family all over the world — everywhere I go. Because my fans really show me the love and I love them just as much.

— *Michael Jackson*

I like birthday cake. It's so symbolic. It's a tempting symbol to load with something more complicated than just "Happy birthday!" because it's this emblem of childhood and a happy day.

— *Aimee Bender*

CHAPTER 5

Gifts

Every birthday is a gift. Every day is a gift.
– Aretha Franklin

When carrying a jar of honey to give to a friend for his birthday, don't stop and eat it along the way.

– Joan Powers, Pooh's Little Instruction Book (1995)

A happy birthday is measured not in the amount of gifts one gets, but in the amount love one receives.

– Todd Stocker

The question on my husband's birthday is always, "What do you get for the man who has nothing?"

– Pamela Druckerman

Handmade presents are scary because they reveal that you have too much free time.

— *Douglas Coupland*

Don't expect gifts on your birthday because when you were born you already received the greatest gift, existence!

— *Mehmet Murat ildan*

Love the giver more than the gift.

— *Brigham Young*

I'm not really big on gifts. I like giving back on my birthday.

— *Liza Soberano*

I think, at a child's birth, if a mother could ask a fairy godmother to endow it with the most useful gift, that gift should be curiosity.

— *Eleanor Roosevelt*

For my fifth birthday, I got a small tennis racket. That's how I started.

— *Ana Ivanovic*

On my fourth or fifth birthday, a guitar was given to me, and I made a new friend. A very loud friend.

— Eliot Sumner

When I was six years old, Mom and Dad gave me a guitar for my birthday, and Daddy taught me the chords to "You Are My Sunshine."

— Roy Orbison

When I was six, my best friend's parents bought him a piano. My mother noticed that every time I would go to his house, the first thing I would say to him was "Levester" – his name was Levester – I said, "Levester, can I go play your piano?" So, on my 7th birthday, my parents bought me a piano.

— Herbie Hancock

I saw these little trucks that I was obsessed with, and my dad got me one for my eighth birthday. That was the start of my racing career.

— Hailie Deegan

A family friend was staying with us once and had brought over a ukulele. I just loved the way she played it. I saved up the money from my 11th birthday and went out and bought one for myself.

— Grace VanderWaal

The first guitar I ever got was for my 13th birthday.

– Rick Springfield

✻

I told my father I wanted to play the banjo, and so he saved the money and got ready to give me a banjo for my next birthday. And between that time and my birthday, I lost interest in the banjo and was playing guitar.

– Jackson Browne

✻

When I was 13 or 14, my mother used to gift me books that I was dying to read. Those are my most memorable birthday gifts.

– Kajol

✻

On my 14th birthday, my grandfather and my grandmother gave me the best birthday present ever: a drafting table that I have worked on ever since.

– Jarrett J. Krosoczka

✻

The sexiest thing my girlfriend has ever done for me is when she planned three full days of events, meals, and surprises for my birthday. It was like one continuous gift.

– Chris Wood

✻

I played rugby for years, and I had a rugby jacket that I lost when I was 14. Somehow, my brother found it in storage 15 years later, and he gave it back to me for my 30th birthday. That was amazing and probably one of the best gifts I've ever received.

— *Ryan Reynolds*

To give somebody your time is the biggest gift you can give.

— *Franka Potente*

On my 30th birthday, all the presents I got were boxes of food. That's what I needed.

— *Kay Lenz*

I want a chainsaw very badly, because I think cutting down a tree would be unbelievably satisfying. I have asked for a chainsaw for my birthday, but I think I'll probably be given jewelry instead.

— *Susan Orlean*

I just had my 30th birthday and we went turkey shooting. It's what I wanted to do, so we went.

— *Kelly Clarkson*

There are three hundred and sixty-four days when you might get un-birthday presents, and only one for birthday presents, you know.

— *Lewis Carroll*

⚮

I'm scared of heights, but for my 30th birthday I'm going to try and get someone to kick me out of a plane and do a parachute jump.

— *Kell Brook*

⚮

I'm not materialistic. I believe in presents from the heart, like a drawing that a child does.

— *Victoria Beckham*

⚮

If you can give your child only one gift, let it be enthusiasm.

— *U.S. Representative Bruce Barton*

⚮

On every birthday, I ask my wife, "What would you like this year?" and her instant reply is, "Diamonds! Diamonds! Diamonds!" I'm always living in hope that one day she'll say she just wants me!

— *Akshay Kumar*

⚮

For my birthday, my husband learned to cook and is cooking one day a week for me. But he only likes to do fancy dishes. So, we end up with weird, obscure things in the refrigerator.

— *Cheryl Hines*

⚮

For my 50th birthday, my cousin Helmut gave me the most profound, beautiful, and striking present. He made books out of my dad's
slide photographs, which were stored and forgotten. Looking at those
books made me cry.

— Juergen Teller

❧

All I want for my birthday is another birthday.

— Ian Dury

❧

I have given myself a Tesla for my 60th birthday.

— Stanley Druckenmiller

❧

I have had fans make me the big picture collages of the photo books; I
have had fans send me birthday cakes… sing to me on my voicemail.
I have had fans flash me. I have had older fans give me their bras and
underwear onstage.

— Sean Puffy Combs

❧

My great-grandmother lived to be 100 years old, so I got to know her.
She always sent us birthday cards that had $2 bills inside; we kept
them for good luck.

— White House Press Secretary Dana Perino

❧

I thought it would be cool to Skype with fans on their birthday and spend, like, a half-hour with them. I did a couple of two-hour Skypes. I just hang out with them and play songs and stuff. At first they're kind of shy, but after a while they open up. I've had a lot of people tell me I'm doing something no one has ever done before.

– *Austin Mahone*

The main prank that we play with props is for people's birthdays. The special effects people will put a little explosive in the cake so it blows up in their face – that's always fun to play on a guest star, or one of the trainees or someone who's new.

– *Catherine Bell*

Your children need your presence more than your presents.

– *Jesse Jackson*

One time for my birthday, mom and dad bought me an acting course 'cause I've always liked the performance side of anything.

– *Zoe Bell*

My mom's always asking me for hits and stolen bases and home runs and different things on Mother's Day and her birthday.

– *Major League Baseball Player Trea Turner*

One thing that was really dope for me was that my dad had a '78 Corvette, '78 or '76 Corvette all my life. It always needed to be fixed up. I remember it's just been sitting in the driveway for years, and I got it fixed from top to bottom for his birthday.

— *Sevyn Streeter*

I used to go to musicals every birthday – that was my birthday present. We'd go to London, me and my two brothers and mum and dad. I think I saw "Mamma Mia" about five times.

— *Lily James*

Every birthday my wife Kathy re-creates what my mom made me on my birthday, a simple pot roast that she slathers with cream of mushroom and Lipton Onion soup and then simmers it all day on the stove.

— *Steve Doocy*

I love getting scared. I find myself putting myself in situations like haunted houses or going to a haunted hospital for my birthday. Yes, I've actually done that.

— *Selena Gomez*

The most important thing you can give to someone on their birthday is your undivided attention and super positive compliments. For one day let us just forget with what's wrong with them or with the world and be positive just for a day. That's one good way to celebrate a birthday.

— *Sarvesh Jain*

God gave us the gift of life; it is up to us to give ourselves the gift of living well.

— *Voltaire*

I've got some incredible fans actually - so loyal and they make me birthday cards and Christmas cards. I got this package of poems and artwork based around the songs. They've got this thing called "Floetry" where they all have to put in artwork. They've set up their own competitions and stuff which is kind of amazing.

— *Florence Welch*

A gift consists not in what is done or given, but in the intention of the giver or doer.

— *Lucius Annaeus Seneca*

Which is why mimes are rarely invited to birthday parties, as the gifts they gave were usually invisible boxes.

— *J.S. Mason, A Dragon, A Pig, and a Rabbi Walk into a Bar... and other Rambunctious Bites (2021)*

The greatest gift that you can give to others is the gift of unconditional love and acceptance.

— *Brian Tracy*

The manner of giving is worth more than the gift.

— *Pierre Corneille*

My wife and I love to travel, so if we don't have work on either her or my birthday, we definitely travel.

— *Barun Sobti*

My mom FedExes a red velvet cake she makes from scratch to me every birthday.

— *Molly Sims*

In 1993, my birthday present was a star on Hollywood's Walk of Fame.

— *Annette Funicello*

A gift, with a kind countenance, is a double present.

— *Thomas Fuller*

A friend never defends a husband who gets his wife an electric skillet for her birthday.

— *Erma Bombeck*

＊

Presents don't really mean much to me. I don't want to sound mawkish, but — it was the realization that I have a great many people in my life who really love me, and who I really love.

— *Gabriel Byrne*

＊

When I was young and it was someone's birthday, I didn't have the money to buy nice presents so I would take my mom's camera and make a movie parody for whoever's birthday it was. When I'd show it them, they'd die laughing. That reaction was a high for me, and I loved that feeling.

— *David Henrie*

＊

You take away all the other luxuries in life, and if you can make someone smile and laugh, you have given the most special gift: happiness.

— *Brad Garrett*

＊

The greatest gifts you can give your children are the roots of responsibility and the wings of independence.

— *Denis Waitley*

＊

The Birthday travels patiently and silently to inspire and aspire happiness, with the gifts of surprise and love of family and friends.

— *Ehsan Sehgal*

Everyone who reaches a milestone birthday in their lives has an opportunity to truly appreciate the fact that presumably we have acquired all the gifts that maturity and age can bring us.

— *Judith Durham*

CHAPTER 6

Milestones

> **Forty is the old age of youth; fifty is the youth of old age.**
> — *French Senator Victor Hugo*

It was on my fifth birthday that Papa put his hand on my shoulder and said, "Remember, my son, if you ever need a helping hand, you'll find one at the end of your arm."

— *Sam Levenson*

That is one of the advantages of being thirteen. You know so much more than you did when you were only twelve.

— *Lucy Maud Montgomery, Anne of Green Gables (1908)*

You're seventeen now. You can do... absolutely nothing you couldn't already.

— *Abby McDonald, Getting Over Garrett Delaney (2012)*

The joy and heartache of an 18th birthday from a mother's heart. Extremely proud, yet fragile feelings with bountiful heartfelt memories of all the joy you bring each day. I love you with all my heart and want everything for you and more. Bless this world with your joyful presence, as you share your gifts in this world.

— *Virginia Toole*

At 19, everything is possible and tomorrow looks friendly.

— *Jim Bishop*

At twenty-one, so many things appear solid, permanent, untenable.

— *Orson Welles*

Thirty was so strange for me. I've really had to come to terms with the fact that I am now a walking and talking adult.

— *C.S. Lewis*

A man thirty years old, I said to myself, should have his field of life all ploughed, and his planting well done; for after that it is summer time.

— *New Mexico Territorial Governor Lew Wallace*

All that I know I learned after I was thirty.

— *French Prime Minister Georges Clemenceau*

It is well for the world that in most of us, by the age of thirty, the character has set like plaster, and will never soften again.

– *William James*

Life really does begin at forty. Up until then, you are just doing research.

– *Carl Gustav Jung*

We don't understand life any better at forty than at twenty, but we know it and admit it.

– *Jules Renard*

Life begins at 40 – but so do fallen arches, rheumatism, faulty eyesight, and the tendency to tell a story to the same person, three or four times.

– *Helen Rowland*

The lovely thing about being forty is that you can appreciate twenty-five-year-old men more.

– *Colleen McCullough*

Every man over forty is a scoundrel.

– *George Bernard Shaw*

A man of forty today has nothing to worry him but falling hair, inability to button the top button, failing vision, shortness of breath, a tendency of the collar to shut off all breathing, trembling of the kidneys to whatever tune the orchestra is playing, and a general sense of giddiness when the matter of rent is brought up. Forty is Life's Golden Age.

— *Robert Benchley*

After forty, a woman has to choose between losing her figure or her face. My advice is to keep your face, and stay sitting down.

— *Barbara Cartland*

Men who have reached and passed forty-five, have a look as if waiting for the secret of the other world, and as if they were perfectly sure of having found out the secret of this.

— *Israeli Prime Minister Golda Meir*

At 50, you need to laugh about your age. If you don't, everybody else will do it for you.

— *Helen Hayes*

By the time we hit fifty, we have learned our hardest lessons. We have found out that only a few things are really important. We have learned to take life seriously, but never ourselves.

— *Marie Dressler*

There's nothing stressful about turning 50 except people reminding you about it.

— *Muhammad Ali*

There's nothing stressful about turning 50 except people reminding you about it.

At fifty the madwoman in the attic breaks loose, stomps down the stairs, and sets fire to the house. She won't be imprisoned anymore.

— *Erica Jong*

Maybe it's true that life begins at fifty. But everything else starts to wear out, fall out, or spread out.

— *Phyllis Diller*

At fifty, everyone has the face he deserves.

— *George Orwell*

The real sadness of fifty is not that you change so much, but that you change so little.

— *Max Lerner*

When you're 50, you start thinking about things you haven't thought about before. I used to think getting old was about vanity – but actually it's about losing people you love. Getting wrinkles is trivial.

— *Eugene O'Neill*

One of the shocks of a 50th birthday is realizing the fundamental fact that your youth is irrevocably over.

— *Marianne Williamson*

After fifty, one ceases to digest. As someone once said, "I just ferment my food now."

— *Henry Green*

A man who views the world the same at fifty as he did at twenty has wasted thirty years of his life.

— *Muhammad Ali*

The heyday of woman's life is the shady side of fifty.

— *Elizabeth Cady Stanton*

The years between fifty and seventy are the hardest. You are always being asked to do things, and yet you are not decrepit enough to turn them down.

— *George Eliot*

With sixty staring me in the face, I have developed inflammation of the sentence structure and definite hardening of the paragraphs.

— *James Thurber*

I wanted to show I had balls at age 60. Just because society says I'm old, doesn't mean that I am. I'm pursuing happiness, even if it makes the people around me unhappy.

— *Sylvester Stallone*

❈

If I had to live again I would do exactly the same thing. Of course I have regrets, but if you are 60 years old and you have no regrets then you haven't lived.

— *Christy Moore*

❈

At sixty, a man has passed most of the reefs and whirlpools. That man has awakened to a new youth. Ergo, he is young.

— *George Luks*

❈

A man of sixty has spent twenty years in bed and over three years in eating.

— *Arnold Bennett*

❈

I was born old and get younger every day. At present I am sixty years young.

— *Herbert Beerbohm Tree*

❈

One starts to get young at the age of sixty and then it is too late.

— *Pablo Picasso*

❈

Life has got to be lived – that's all there is to it. At seventy, I would say the advantage is that you take life more calmly. You know that "this, too, shall pass!"

  – Eleanor Roosevelt

I did two things on my seventy-fifth birthday. I visited my wife's grave. Then I joined the army.

Visiting Kathy's grave was the less dramatic of the two.

  – John Scalzi, Old Man's War (2005)

The advantage of being eighty years old is that one has many people to love.

  – Jean Renoir

CHAPTER 7

Fountain of Youth

> **The secret of staying young is to live honestly,
> eat slowly, and lie about your age.**
> *— Lucille Ball*

Youth is a wonderful thing. What a crime to waste it on children.

— George Bernard Shaw

Youre only young once, but you can be immature forever.

— Germaine Greer

Anyone who stops learning is old, whether at twenty or eighty. Anyone who keeps learning stays young. The greatest thing in life is to keep your mind young.

— Henry Ford

There is a fountain of youth: it is your mind, your talents, the creativity you bring to your life and the lives of the people you love. When you learn to tap this source, you will truly have defeated age.

— *Sophia Loren*

Youth is a circumstance you can't do anything about. The trick is to grow up without getting old.

— *Frank Lloyd Wright*

Youth has no age.

— *Pablo Picasso*

Those whom the gods love grow young.

— *Oscar Wilde*

Youth is a disease from which we all recover.

— *Dorothy Fuldheim*

Youth would be an ideal state if it came a little later in life.

— *British Prime Minister H.H. Asquith*

To me, fair friend, you never can be old. For as you were when first your eye I ey'd, such seems your beauty still.

    — William Shakespeare

∞

Youth comes but once in a lifetime.

    — Henry Wadsworth Longfellow

∞

Keep true to the dream of thy youth.

    — Friedrich Von Schiller

∞

For the youth, the indignation of most things will just surge as each birthday passes.

    — Chris Evans

∞

Youth had been a habit of hers for so long that she could not part with it.

    — Rudyard Kipling

∞

You can't put off being young until you retire.

    — Philip Larkin

∞

It takes a long time to become young.

    — Pablo Picasso

∞

CHAPTER 8

Long in the Tooth

> **To me, old age is always 10 years older than I am.**
> *– Elder Statesman Bernard Baruch*

Inside every older person is a younger person wondering what the hell happened.

– Cora Harvey Armstrong

You know you are getting old when people tell you how good you look.

– Alan King

I don't feel old. I don't feel anything till noon. That's when it's time for my nap.

– Bob Hope

I still think of myself as I was 25 years ago. Then I look in a mirror and see an old bastard, and I realize it's me.

– *Dave Allen*

My faculties are decaying now and soon I shall be so I cannot remember any but the things that never happened.

– *Mark Twain*

On my 50th birthday in 2005, my discount-wielding AARP card came in the mail. I hurled it in the trash, put on something fabulous, and had a decadent meal. Just the thought of putting it in my wallet felt like a concession.

– *Iman*

When grace is joined with wrinkles, it is adorable. There is an unspeakable dawn in happy old age.

– *French Senator Victor Hugo*

None are so old as those who have outlived enthusiasm.

– *Henry David Thoreau*

At my age flowers scare me.

– *George Burns*

The more sand has escaped from the hourglass of our life, the clearer we should see through it.

— *Niccolo Machiavelli*

My first recognition of age setting in was exactly on my 36th birthday. I have no idea why, on this day of all days, I looked in the mirror and realized my face no longer looked young.

— *Paulina Porizkova*

Life is like a hot bath. It feels good while you're in it, but the longer you stay, the more wrinkled you get.

— *Jim Davis*

Time may be a great healer, but it's a lousy beautician.

— *Dorothy Parker*

I'd be happy to live till 80 as long as I was comfortable and in good health. Mind you, ask me again on the eve of my 80th birthday. Even so, I hope we don't all start living to be 120. I'm not sure I'd cope with another 60 years.

— *Bonnie Tyler*

The older the fiddler, the sweeter the tune.

— *Pope Paul VI*

Old age is the time when birthday candles cost more than the birthday cake itself, and half of your urine is wasted on medical testing.

– *Faina Ranevskaya*

❈

Some people try to turn back their odometers. Not me, I want people to know why I look this way. I've traveled a long way and some of the roads weren't paved.

– *Will Rogers*

❈

I'm very accepting with my age. It's like notches on your belt: experience, wisdom, and a different kind of beauty. There comes a day when you've become comfortable in your skin.

– *Zoe Saldana*

❈

No wise man ever wished to be younger.

– *Jonathan Swift*

❈

Old age is a shipwreck.

– *French President Charles de Gaulle*

❈

Nobody grows old merely by living a number of years. We grow old by deserting our ideals. Years may wrinkle the skin, but to give up enthusiasm wrinkles the soul.

– *Samuel Ullman*

❈

With mirth and laughter let old wrinkles come.

— *William Shakespeare*

To know how to grow old is the masterwork of wisdom, and one of the most difficult chapters in the great art of living.

— *Henri Frederic Amiel*

If you survive long enough, you're revered – rather like an old building.

— *Katherine Hepburn*

The paradox of life; everyone desires a fuller life. But no one wishes to increase in age.

— *Lailah Gifty Akita*

I don't pay attention to the number of birthdays. It's weird when I say I'm 53. It just is crazy that I'm 53. I think I'm very immature. I feel like a kid. That's why my back goes out all the time, because I completely forget I can't do certain things anymore – like doing the plank for 10 minutes.

— *Ellen DeGeneres*

Live your life and forget your age.

— *Norman Vincent Peale*

First you forget names, then you forget faces. Next you forget to pull your zipper up and finally, you forget to pull it down.

— *George Burns*

Old age has its pleasures, which, though different, are not less than the pleasures of youth.

— *W. Somerset Maugham*

Let us respect gray hairs, especially our own.

— *J.P. Sears*

Old age is not a matter for sorrow. It is matter for thanks if we have left our work done behind us.

— *Thomas Carlyle*

To be happy, we must be true to nature and carry our age along with us.

— *William Hazlitt*

Age is a high price to pay for maturity.

— *Tom Stoppard*

Old people are fond of giving good advice; it consoles them for no longer being capable of setting a bad example.

    — Francois de La Rochefoucauld

I'm amazed. When I was 40, I thought I'd never make 50. And at 50 I thought the frosting on the cake would be 60. At 60, I was still going strong and enjoying everything.

    — Gloria Stuart

Old age deprives the intelligent man only of qualities useless to wisdom.

    — Joseph Joubert

Just remember, once you're over the hill you begin to pick up speed.

    — Arthur Schopenhauer

Our wrinkles are our medals of the passage of life. They are what we have been through and who we want to be.

    — Lauren Hutton

Old age is like everything else. To make a success of it, you've got to start young.

    — President Theodore Roosevelt

To keep the heart unwrinkled, to be hopeful, kindly, cheerful, reverent – that is to triumph over old age.

— *Thomas Bailey Aldrich*

❈

Old age: the crown of life, our play's last act.

— *Roman Statesman Marcus Tullius Cicero*

❈

Please don't retouch my wrinkles. It took me so long to earn them.

— *Anna Magnani*

❈

Error is acceptable as long as we are young; but one must not drag it along into old age.

— *Johann Wolfgang von Goethe*

❈

You will recognize, my boy, the first sign of old age: it is when you go out into the streets of London and realize for the first time how young the policemen look.

— *Seymour Hicks*

❈

You know how to tell when you're getting old? When your broad mind changes places with your narrow waist.

— *Red Skelton*

❈

Grow old along with me! The best is yet to be.

— *Robert Browning*

You'll find as you grow older that you weren't born such a great while ago after all. The time shortens up.

— *William Dean Howells*

Pretend to be dumb, that's the only way to reach old age.

— *Friedrich Durrenmatt*

I have the problems of, I must confess, old age.

— *Billy Graham*

One compensation of old age is that it excuses you from picnics.

— *William Feather*

Cherish all your happy moments; they make a fine cushion for old age.

— *Indiana State Representative Booth Tarkington*

After you're older, two things are possibly more important than any others: health and money.

— *Helen Gurley Brown*

Discussing how old you are is the temple of boredom.

— *Ruth Gordon*

The secret of genius is to carry the spirit of the child into old age, which means never losing your enthusiasm.

— *Aldous Huxley*

We have to be able to grow up. Our wrinkles are our medals of the passage of life. They are what we have been through and who we want to be.

— *Lauren Hutton*

I am long on ideas, but short on time. I expect to live to be only about a hundred.

— *Thomas Edison*

You'll live to be a hundred if you give up all the things that make you want to.

— *Woody Allen*

Old age is not for sissies.

— *New Jersey State Senator Malcolm Forbes*

They tell you that you'll lose your mind when you grow older. What they don't tell you is that you won't miss it very much.

— *Malcolm Cowley*

CHAPTER 9

Lifecycle

> **You've heard of the three ages of man – youth, age, and "you are looking wonderful."**
> – *Francis Cardinal Spellman*

From our birthday, until we die, is but the winking of an eye.

— *Irish Free State Senator William Butler Yeats*

From birth to age eighteen, a girl needs good parents. From eighteen to thirty-five, she needs good looks. From thirty-five to fifty-five, she needs a good personality. From fifty-five on, she needs good cash.

— *Sophie Tucker*

Youth is the gift of nature, but age is the work of art.

— *Stanislaw Jerzy Lec*

When you are younger you get blamed for crimes you never committed, and when you're older you begin to get credit for virtues you never possessed. It evens itself out.

 — *Baseball Hall of Famer Casey Stengel*

Rashness belongs to youth; prudence to old age.

 — *Roman Statesman Marcus Tullius Cicero*

It's an epitome of life. The first half of it consists of the capacity to enjoy without the chance; the last half consists of the chance without the capacity.

 — *Mark Twain*

In youth we learn; in age we understand.

 — *Marie von Ebner-Eschenbach*

Youth is the time for adventures of the body, but age for the triumphs of the mind.

 — *Logan Pearsall Smith*

Youth is a blunder,

Manhood a struggle,

Old Age a regret.

> *— British Prime Minister Benjamin Disraeli*

At fifteen, my mind was bent on learning.

At thirty, I stood firm.

At forty, I had no doubts.

At fifty, I knew the decrees of Heaven.

At sixty, my ear was receptive to truth.

At seventy, I could follow my heart's desires without sin.

> *— Confucius*

At twenty years of age, the will reigns; at thirty, the wit; and at forty, the judgement.

> *— U.S. Founding Father Benjamin Franklin*

Middle age is when you still believe you'll feel better in the morning.

> *— Bob Hope*

Middle age is when you're faced with two temptations and you choose the one that will get you home by nine o'clock.

— *President Ronald Reagan*

Of middle age, the best that can be said is that a middle-aged person has likely learned how to have a little fun in spite of his troubles.

— *Don Marquis*

Middle age: when you begin to exchange your emotions for symptoms.

— *Irvin S. Cobb*

Perhaps middle age is, or should be, a period of shedding shells; the shell of ambition, the shell of material accumulations and possessions, the shell of the ego.

— *Anne Morrow Lindbergh*

The really frightening thing about middle age is the knowledge that you'll grow out of it.

— *Doris Day*

Middle age occurs when you are too young to take up golf and too old to rush up to the net.

— *Franklin P. Adams*

Middle age is when your age starts to show around your middle.

— *Bob Hope*

Middle age is when your classmates are so gray, wrinkled, and bald they don't recognize you.

— *Bennett Cerf*

The first forty years of our life give the text, the next thirty furnish the commentary upon it, which enables us rightly to understand the true meaning and connection of the text with its moral and its beauties.

— *Arthur Schopenhauer*

To my surprise, my 70s are nicer than my 60s and my 60s than my 50s, and I wouldn't wish my teens and 20s on my enemies.

— *Lionel Blue*

In childhood, we yearn to be grown-ups. In old age, we yearn to be kids. It just seems that all would be wonderful if we didn't have to celebrate our birthdays in chronological order.

— *Robert Breault*

The old believe everything; the middle-aged suspect everything; the young know everything.

    – Oscar Wilde

It is utterly false and cruelly arbitrary... to put all the play and learning into childhood, all the work into middle age, and all the regrets into old age.

    – Margaret Mead

Life would be infinitely happier if we could only be born at the age of eighty and gradually approach eighteen.

    – Mark Twain

CHAPTER 10

Fragapanophobia

(Fear of Birthdays)

> **I hate birthdays, did you know too
> many can actually kill you?**
> *– Nitya Prakash*

Every human's birth starts with crying; it becomes its birthday every year; one celebrates it with dears and cheers, one with fears and tears.

– Ehsan Sehgal

I have this PTSD from a birthday party where no one showed up.

– Emily Hampshire

I hate birthdays. I thought that I only hated my own birthday, and then I realized that I hate my children's birthdays too.

– Samantha Bee

Well, birthdays are merely symbolic of how another year has gone by and how little we've grown. No matter how desperate we are that someday a better self will emerge, with each flicker of the candles on the cake, we know it's not to be, that for the rest of our sad, wretched pathetic lives, this is who we are to the bitter end. Inevitably, irrevocably; happy birthday? No such thing.

– Jerry Seinfeld

I like to go to anybody else's birthday, and if I'm invited, I'm a good guest. But I never celebrate my birthdays. I really don't care.

– Mikhail Baryshnikov

I wish people would stop talking about my birthday.

– George Bernard Shaw

I get uncomfortable when people give me presents and watch me open them. I don't have birthday parties, because the idea of a group of people singing and looking at me while I'm blowing out candles gives me hives.

– Brit Marling

Anybody can have a birthday. It requires nothing. Murderers have birthdays. It's the opposite of anything that I believe in. And I don't like at work where you stop everything to sing 'Happy Birthday' to someone. I feel like that's for children.

– *Mindy Kaling*

As soon as I became a mom, my birthday stopped having any meaning whatsoever.

– *Marisol Nichols*

If you're extremely, painfully frightened of age, it shows.

– *Jeanne Moreau*

"We do have funerals for the living," Jill said. "They're called birthday parties."

– *Andrew Shaffer, Hope Never Dies (2018)*

I don't know anyone that doesn't get emotional around their birthday.

– *Alana Haim*

I'm in a difficult position in the sense that, preposterous as this might sound, I don't like being the center of attention. I get up on stage every night and play songs, but I almost feel the songs are the center of attention. I don't like opening my birthday presents in front of people, either.

– *Alex Turner*

You know how most people dread a birthday. Well, I feel the exact opposite. I feel that every day is an extraordinary gift. Just to be here, and especially to be here with you.

– *James Patterson, Suzanne's Diary for Nicholas (2001)*

Now that I think about it, my 40th birthday was the most anxiety I've ever had, and my wedding was also the second time I've had that much anxiety. So, I'm starting to realize that I can't be throwing these big bash parties because I need to own that I get anxiety with a lot of people diverting their attention to me.

– *Jeannie Mai*

I'm not a big birthday guy; I never have been.

– *Lewis Black*

I miss my mom and dad. They brought me into this world, and I wish they were with me on my birthday. So, I don't celebrate it much.

– *Sonu Sood*

I'm not going to be caught around here for any fool celebration. To hell with birthdays!

– *Norman Rockwell*

I'm going to hide – I always do on my birthday. I never celebrate birthdays.

– *Laila Rouass*

I'm not a birthday person. Maybe because I don't like to build expectations around that one day. You never know how it'll turn out to be.

– *Ranbir Kapoor*

I hate my birthday. I don't like to celebrate it much. But, if someone wants to throw me a surprise party, that normally works better.

– *Sophie*

I hate birthdays. I hate birthday parties. I hate them. I don't know what it is, anybody's only got to come wafting near me with a piece of cake with a candle on and I break out in hives.

– *Cat Deeley*

Don't regret another birthday, the good news is that you are alive and can celebrate it.

– *Catherine Pulsifer*

A birthday is not a day to fear. It is a day to celebrate and look forward to the coming year.

– *Byron Pulsifer*

CHAPTER 11

Religious Teachings

Your birthday is a reminder that God gave you life. It gives you a fresh start every year. It symbolizes the fact that there was something about God's image that He wanted to create in you and share with the world.

— *Sadie Robertson, Live (2020)*

I know when I was born, but I don't know when I will go. No matter what, I thank God.

— *Egba Terry*

Because time itself is like a spiral, something special happens on your birthday each year: The same energy that God invested in you at birth is present once again.

— *Menachem Mendel Schneerson*

Birthdays are special days. It reminds us of that day when the heavens gave miracles our way. You are a MIRACLE. Bless yourself. Bless others. Be a blessing.

— *Mystqx Skye*

The universe wanted you to celebrate and appreciate your life so every year she gave you a birthday.

— *Dr. Debasish Mridha*

We love the illusion of birthdays every year, but ignore the reality [of] death. If death ends the story absolutely, it is unreasonable to celebrate the day of birth. If death is the real beginning of Eternal life, isn't it even more unreasonable to celebrate a day which leads us to death and fear the day which leads us to life?

— *Ajay Chandan*

Did you know that Christmas means "Christ" (Jesus) and "mas" (a celebration)? The story about Jesus is found in the name of that special day when we celebrate His birth!

— *USVI Superior Court Judge Soraya Diase Coffelt*

The day which we fear as our last is but the birthday of eternity.

— *Seneca the Younger*

Plant the seeds of love in your hearts. Let them grow into trees of service and shower the sweet fruit of Ananda. Share the Ananda with all. That is the proper way to celebrate the birthday.

— *Sathya Sai Baba*

I ask you to pray for me, for once age has overtaken us, we find consolation only in religion.

— *Paul Cezanne*

My father was a Shaman. He told me that time doesn't exist. He didn't use a clock. He didn't know when my birthday was.

— *Alessandro Michele*

Our brains are seventy-year clocks. The Angel of Life winds them up once for all, then closes the case, and gives the key into the hand of the Angel of the Resurrection.

— *Oliver Wendell Holmes, Sr.*

Except ye become as little children, except you can wake on your fiftieth birthday with the same forward-looking excitement and interest in life that you enjoyed when you were five, "ye cannot enter the kingdom of God." One must not only die daily, but every day we must be born again.

— *Dorothy L. Sayers*

As I approached my 95th birthday, I was burdened to write a book that addressed the epidemic of "easy believism." There is a mindset today that if people believe in God and do good works, they are going to Heaven.

– *Billy Graham*

His sons used to hold feasts in their homes on their birthdays, and they would invite their three sisters to eat and drink with them.

– *Job 1:4, Holy Bible (New International Version)*

The glory of young men is their strength, gray hair the splendor of the old.

– *Proverbs 20:29, Holy Bible (New International Version)*

CHAPTER 12

Miscellaneous

> **You were born an original. Don't die a copy.**
> — *John Mason*

The best birthdays of all are those that haven't arrived yet.

— *Robert Orben*

It is lovely, when I forget all birthdays, including my own, to find that somebody remembers me.

— *Ellen Glasgow*

When you wake up every day, it's like a new birthday: it's a new chance to be great again and make great decisions.

— *Poo Bear*

Need a life hack? Celebrate people's birthday more than they want to. You can never celebrate too much.

– *Sarvesh Jain*

⧝

Birthday should be considered as a unit of measurement to measure our present status toward success!

– *Mohith Agadi*

⧝

It is not how old you are, but how you are old.

– *Marie Dressler*

⧝

I'm lost in the middle of my birthday. I want my friends, their touch, with the earth's last love. I will take life's final offering. I will take the last human blessing.

– *Rabindranath Tagore*

⧝

My son told me to stop singing "Happy Birthday" when he was four.

– *Dr. Ruth Westheimer*

⧝

A man's as old as he's feeling. A woman as old as she looks.

– *Samuel Taylor Coleridge*

⧝

I always knew that good stuff would come along when I was older. So, when I was 18, I longed to be 30; when I was 30, I longed to be 50. I've always looked forward to my next birthday.

— *Joanna Lumley*

Entrepreneurs don't have weekends or birthdays or holidays. Every day is my weekend, my birthday, my holiday. Or, every day is my work day. Mostly it's a choice.

— *Richie Norton*

Birthdays are happy as a child, defeatist with age and joyful again at surviving another year.

— *Stewart Stafford*

Facebook is the digital equivalent of my secretary, or perhaps my wife, yelling at me not to forget to wish someone a happy birthday or to inform me I have a social engagement this evening.

— *Sarah Jeong*

A good man measures his life not in the number of his years, but in the quality of his friends.

— *Todd Stocker*

You are as young as your faith, as old as your doubt; as young as your self-confidence, as old as your fear, as young as your hope, as old as your despair.

— *Samuel Ullman*

Every birthday celebrates a life because every life is important.

— *Richelle E. Goodrich, Slaying Dragons: Quotes, Poetry, & a Few Short Stories for Every Day of the Year (2017)*

I want to feel pampered and special on my birthday.

— *Rashami Desai*

I'm one of those people who had Christmas and my birthday always combined, and generally, my birthday was pretty much ignored. But my parents are always good about making some kind of special effort to make me feel like I also have a birthday that exists.

— *Noel Wells*

A birthday is a good time to begin a new; throwing away the old habits, as you would old clothes, and never putting them on again.

— *Amos Bronson Alcott*

It is not length of life, but depth of life.

— *Ralph Waldo Emerson*

∞

John Candy knew he was going to die. He told me on his 40th birthday. He said, "Well, Maureen. I'm on borrowed time."

— *Maureen O'Hara*

∞

Birthdays could be such a bummer when you were older than the country you lived in.

— *Lynsay Sands, A Quick Bite (2005)*

∞

When I was little, I thought, isn't it nice that everybody celebrates on my birthday? Because it's July 4th.

— *Gloria Stuart*

∞

The longer I live, the less future there is to worry about.

— *Ashleigh Brilliant*

∞

I spend my birthday at home close to the people who matter to me. That's the way I like it.

— *Simi Garewal*

∞

A birthday wish granted 23 years late is still a birthday wish granted.

– *R.K. Milholland*

That's the great thing about New Year's, you get to be a year older. For me, that wasn't such a joke, because my birthday was always around this time. When I was a kid, my father used to tell me that everybody was celebrating my birthday. That's what the trees are all about.

– *Alan King*

March 15th is the most important day of the year. It's my birthday.

– *Maxwell Jacob Friedman*

I am a birthday person. I am not modest about birthdays.

– *Parineeti Chopra*

I don't go into a fight mad. I go into a fight like it's my birthday. I love what I'm doing.

– *Paige VanZant*

We grow neither better nor worse as we get old, but more like ourselves.

– *Elder Statesman Bernard Baruch*

Despite her insistence that no one should make a big deal about her birthday, no one ever listened. There was always so much pressure to have the perfect happy day.

— *Michelle Madow, Diamonds are Forever (2015)*

The worst part about celebrating another birthday is the shock that you're only as well as you are.

— *Anne Lamott*

Don't celebrate how old you are, celebrate the years you survived.

— *Touaxia Vang*

It's your birthday today, so what would you say if we turned that frown upside down.

— *Billie Jean King*

I'll sometimes forget it's my birthday, but my mom has taken to calling me at the exact time of my birth, so that'll usually remind me. It was an important moment for me, obviously, but I guess a more memorable one for her.

— *Steve Kornacki*

You always get a special kick on opening day, no matter how many you go through. You look forward to it like a birthday party when you're a kid. You think something wonderful is going to happen.

– *Joe DiMaggio*

✕

Age is not measured by years. Nature does not equally distribute energy. Some people are born old and tired while others are going strong at seventy.

– *Dorothy Thompson*

✕

My birthday is two days before Valentine's Day, so it has always been about that rather than romance.

– *A.J. Odudu*

✕

If someone close to me forgets my birthday, I am heartbroken.

– *Parineeti Chopra*

✕

I think women should start to embrace their age. What's the alternative to getting older? You die. I can't change the day I was born. But I can take care of my skin, my body, my mind, and try to live my life and be happy.

– *Olivia Munn*

✕

The only way that getting older can be a bad thing is if you are not fully living in the moment now.

— *Andrena Sawyer*

I grabbed a pile of dust, and holding it up, foolishly asked for as many birthdays as the grains of dust. I forgot to ask that they be years of youth.

— *Ovid*

I am a very private person, so on my birthday too I will spend a cozy time with my family and a few close friends!

— *Suniel Shetty*

Birthday is just another day. It's loved ones who make it special.

— *Vikrmn: CA Vikram Verma, You By You (2021)*

My birthday is always around Thanksgiving, and I always had to have turkey on my birthday. My mom was always, "Let's celebrate your birthday on Thanksgiving." My other siblings got to have special dinners they liked. I resented turkey. For a long time, I hated turkey. I've kind of gotten over it.

— *Joey Chestnut*

If I have the power to post "Happy Birthday" on someone's Facebook page and make them feel really good, it feels really good to make other people feel really good. I love it. I'm a huge Facebook and Twitter person. And I love talking to my fans. It's fun.

— *Rebecca Mader*

❈

The heart has no wrinkles.

— *French aristocrat Madame de Sévigné*

❈

Rather than see aging as a reason to contract, we should view it as an opportunity to expand. We should make each year of our lives more interesting than the one before.

— *Srinivas Rao*

❈

I like spending time with my family and friends on my birthday.

— *Prabhas*

❈

I binge when I'm happy. When everything is going really well, every day is like I'm at a birthday party.

— *Kirstie Alley*

❈

Beautiful young people are accidents of nature, but beautiful old people are works of art.

— *Eleanor Roosevelt*

If we could be twice young and twice old, we could correct all our mistakes.

— *Euripides*

Birth and Death are the two noblest expressions of bravery.

— *Khalil Gibran*

A birthday is just another day where you go to work and people give you love. Age is just a state of mind, and you are as old as you think you are. You have to count your blessings and be happy.

— *Abhishek Bachchan*

Your birthday is the beginning of your own personal new year. Your first birthday was a beginning, and each new birthday is a chance to begin again, to start over, to take a new grip on life.

— *Wilfred Peterson*

Every day is a birthday; every moment of it is new to us; we are born again, renewed for fresh work and endeavor.

– *Isaac Watts*

❈

I find the best birthday plans are the unplanned ones.

– *Diana Penty*

❈

That's how birthdays were in our house. All hateful charades of pretty clothes, expensive presents, and ugly words.

– *Debbie Howells, The Bones of You (2015)*

❈

Because no one should be alone and sad on their birthday, even if they thought they wanted to be.

– *Sara Barnard, Beautiful Broken Things (2016)*

❈

Romance novels are birthday cake and life is often peanut butter and jelly. I think everyone should have lots of delicious romance novels lying around for those times when the peanut butter of life gets stuck to the roof of your mouth.

– *Janet Evanovich*

❈

Birthdays were made for going wild over the people we think are amazing.

— *Richelle E. Goodrich, Slaying Dragons: Quotes, Poetry, & a Few Short Stories for Every Day of the Year (2017)*

❧

The reason I met my husband was because I remembered a friend's birthday. The moral of the story is: Remember people's birthdays.

— *Julianna Margulies*

❧

Every man and every living being have the same birth day: The birthday of the universe is our real birthday!

— *Mehmet Murat ildan*

❧

Some people won't go the extra mile, and then on their birthday, when no one makes a fuss, they feel neglected and bitter.

— *Anne Lamott*

❧

I see birthdays as a reward for having shown up 365 in a row. It's like getting a badge for attendance.

— *Gina Barreca, If You Lean In, Will Men Just Look Down Your Blouse?: Questions and Thoughts for Loud, Smart Women in Turbulent Times (2016)*

❧

Not knowing my birthday had never seemed strange. I knew I'd been born near the end of September, and each year I picked a day, one that didn't fall on a Sunday because it's no fun spending your birthday in church.

— *Tara Westover*

My father had always told me that my birthday was the first day of spring. Not a specific day of the year, but the feeling – an undercurrent of warmth waking up the earth. The scent of violets. Green in the air, he called it.

— *Erica Bauermeister, The Scent Keeper (2019)*

To divide one's life by years is of course to tumble into a trap set by our own arithmetic. The calendar consents to carry on its dull wall-existence by the arbitrary timetables we have drawn up in consultation with those permanent commuters, Earth and Sun. But we, unlike trees, need grow no annual rings.

— *Clifton Fadiman*

CONCLUSION

> **If everybody was treated like they matter every day, birthdays wouldn't be so special.**
> — *Mokokoma Mokhonoana*

To summarize the above quotes, birthdays are:

1. the perfect time to reflect on the past and look forward to the future,

2. a great opportunity to celebrate with close friends and family,

3. a blessing from God (so be grateful for this annual present),

4. nothing to fear, and

5. an opportunity to commit to a new purpose.

The differing perspectives and advice given on this topic are as numerous as the folks who enjoy eating cake – which explains why it was relatively easy to find the 501 birthday quotes contained in this book.

The bottom line is that birthdays are a gift and a reminder to do something meaningful with the rest of your life. In any case, I hope the quotes above made you laugh and perhaps think a little deeper about this important subject.

But wait, there's more! I saved the best for last. Below is the TOP TEN LIST of my all-time favorite birthday quotes.

10.   When you were born, you cried and the world rejoiced. Live your life so that when you die, the world cries and you rejoice.

– Cherokee proverb

9.   The seven ages of man: spills, drills, thrills, bills, ills, pills and wills.

– Richard J. Needham

8.   The great thing about getting older is that you don't lose all the other ages you've been.

– Madeleine L'Engle

7.   I have achieved my seventy years in the usual way, by sticking strictly to a scheme of life which would kill anybody else. I will offer here, as a sound maxim, this: That we can't reach old age by another man's road.

– Mark Twain

6.   Youth is happy because it has the ability to see beauty. Anyone who keeps the ability to see beauty never grows old.

– Franz Kafka

5.   I intend to live forever. So far, so good.

   – Steven Wright

∞

4.   A man is not old until regrets take the place of dreams.

   – John Barrymore

∞

3.   The best way to remember your wife's birthday is to forget it once.

   – E. Joseph Cossman

∞

2.   I enjoy the celebration of my birthday as much as anyone else does, but I always remember to start my day thanking my mom because she did most of the work the day I came into the world, not to mention all she has done throughout my life that has contributed so much to the woman I am today.

   – Christy Turlington

∞

And my number one all-time favorite birthday quote is...

1.   Fifty years: here's a time when you have to separate yourself from what other people expect of you, and do what you love. Because if you find yourself 50 years old and you aren't doing what you love, then what's the point?

   – Jim Carrey

∞

Lastly, I'll close out this silly book with one final birthday quote for you to ponder:

> **I decided if you're lucky enough to be alive, you should use each birthday to celebrate what your life is about.**
> – *Mary Steenburgen*

LET'S GET CONNECTED

I hope you enjoyed this silly book! If so, **please do two small favors for me right now.**

First, please take a minute to leave a short review of this book on Amazon, Goodreads, or any other website. Online reviews help new readers find this book. Your help in spreading the word about this book is greatly appreciated!

Second, please sign up for my reader's list at www.mikekowis.com/ signup/ so that we can get connected. After you join, I'll occasionally share exclusive giveaways and announcements about my upcoming books and speaking engagements.

If you have any questions or wish to contact me about speaking to your group, I'm just an email away! Feel free to contact me anytime at *mike.kowis.esq@gmail.com.*

Happy Trails!

ACKNOWLEDGEMENTS

This book would not have been possible without the extraordinary help and support of many folks, including my dear family, friends, and fellow authors.

I also want to offer my sincere appreciation to my long-time friend and movie aficionado, Robert Ziggy Parker, for his generous help in refining the testimonials for this book. In case you didn't figure it out, I made them up for my readers' amusement. If you didn't enjoy them, I blame Mr. Parker! If you loved them, I want to thank you in advance and let you know that Ziggy played a big part in making these zingers as humorous as possible.

Last, I want to give special thanks to Robynne Alexander at Damonza for the cover design, interior print formatting, and eBook conversion work.

It takes a skillful and dedicated team to create a book like this, and everyone who participated has my sincere appreciation for their contributions.

ABOUT THE AUTHOR

By day, **Mike Kowis, Esq.**, is a mild-mannered tax attorney at a Fortune 500 company in Texas. By night, he swaps a three-piece suit for a pair of tights and a shiny red cape and then begins his duties as a modern-day SUPERHERO (also known as Adjunct Faculty Member) for one of the largest community colleges in the Lone Star State.

Specifically, Mike has practiced corporate tax law for 27 years, including the last quarter-century at Entergy Services, LLC where he currently serves as Senior Tax Counsel. In addition, he has taught corporate tax and business law classes at Lone Star College-Montgomery since 2001. In his spare time, he writes books and competes in off-road races.

Mike holds a bachelor's degree and two law degrees, including a LL.M. in taxation from Georgetown University Law Center. He lives in the piney woods of East Texas with his family and a rambunctious puppy named Mr. Pickles. His ten nonfiction books are listed below in their order of publication:

1. *Engaging College Students: A Fun and Edgy Guide for Professors* (a college teaching guide with 44 practical tips to engage students in classroom discussions),

2. *14 Steps to Self-Publishing a Book* (a self-publishing guide that has sold over 5,000 copies),

3. *Maximize Your Book Sales With Data Analysis: The Cure for Authorship Analysis Paralysis* (a free Kindle eBook for authors written by Sharon C. Jenkins and myself),

4. *Smart Marketing for Indie Authors: How I Sold my First 1,563 Books and Counting!* (a book marketing guide for newbie authors),

5. *Texas Off-road Racing: A Father-Son Journey to a Side-by-Side Championship* (the true story of off-road racing with my teenage son during our run for the 2019 Championship of a local cross-country series),

6. *American Tax Triva: The Ultimate Quiz on U.S. Taxation*, (250 fun-filled trivia questions about the fascinating history of U.S. tax law, the IRS, tax forms, and much more),

7. *Texas Off-road Racing 2: The Battle for ATV and Side-by-Side Championships* (this sequel shares the gritty details of ATV and side-by-side racing during Mike's run for the 2022 Championships of a new cross-country series),

8. *The Little Black Book of Tax Wisdom: Quotes, Quips, & Quiddities Every Tax Advisor Should Know* (a huge collection of amusing tax quotes from Mark Twain, Chris Rock, Ronald Reagan, Winston Churchill, George Washington, Judge Learned Hand, David Letterman, and many more),

9. *The Little Black Book of Retirement Wisdom: Amusing Quotes for Retirees* (a riveting collection of humorous and thought-provoking retirement quotes from Betty White, Elon Musk, Mark Twain, Brett Favre, Joan Rivers, Dr. Dre, Billy Graham, George Foreman, and many more), and

10. *The Little Black Book of Birthday Wisdom*: *Quotes on Aging, Life, and Birthday Cake* (a fun collection of amusing quotes about aging, life, and birthday cake from Jerry Seinfeld, Abraham Lincoln, Oprah Winfrey, Sylvestor Stallone, Mark Twain, George Burns, Betty White, and many more).

If you have any questions or would like Mike to speak at an upcoming event, please email him at mike.kowis.esq@gmail.com, find his author page on Facebook (Mike Kowis, Esq.), or visit his website at www. mikekowis.com.

www.ingramcontent.com/pod-product-compliance
Lightning Source LLC
Chambersburg PA
CBHW060243030426
42335CB00014B/1584